with love
& thanks.

June 2015.

MIND'S EYE

MIND'S EYE

A Vision into the Depth of Consciousness

A Collection of Personal Poems

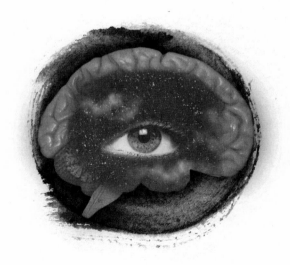

ONALY A. KAPASI, MD

Library of Congress Control Number:		2014908294
ISBN:		
	Hardcover	978-1-4990-1422-8
	Softcover	978-1-4990-1423-5
	eBook	978-1-4990-1420-4

This book was printed in the United States of America.

Rev. date: 05/28/2014

To order additional copies of this book, contact:
Xlibris LLC
1-888-795-4274
www.Xlibris.com
Orders@Xlibris.com
550915

Contents

Special thanks to Shamim Rampuri for the art work

My utmost gratitude to those who have shaped my life

My Mum and Dad

My family

My gurus

and

My friends and foes

A Tribute to My Love

Chandermukhi, my wife

Her skin white translucent alabaster
Her doe eyes an envy of the Buddha
Her gait that of a swan
Her lips petals of dark pink rose

Proud as a peacock
Gentler than a lamb
Voice of the *Koyal*
Her breath a fragrance of musk

Cascade of jet-black hair
Sparkle in the eyes, a glint of mischief
Pearly white teeth
Her heart-piercing smile

We all perceive visual pictures much beyond our physical sight. This perception beyond the physical vision is referred to as the Mind's eye

Poetry is an art form that explores the inner depths of our thoughts. I believe that poetry transports us outside the realm of reality.

Is That God

In the quiet of my life I see with the eye of my soul

My mind reaches places my eye has not seen

There is bliss in the unknown land

Diffuse warmth of a different kind

I am face to face with Him

His light is in my soul, a million sparks all at once

I am not afraid as I and He are one for one timeless moment

I conceived and read the above lines at a wake of a dear family friend

The daughter later remarked that it gave her a feeling of peace, that her mother was now with her Maker

The bliss in the perception within our mind's eye is fathomless. The dimensions are much greater than reality. Meditation I believe hones our ability to perceive beyond our physical sight—to feel beyond sight and touch. An exploration into the depths of our inner consciousness is seeing with the "eye of the mind."

Evolution

Each turn I took
Each new direction I chose
My destination seemed to elude me
I got near but unable to attain my goal

My path became more arduous
I relented but persevered
I prayed for the sight of light
But I only stumbled in darkness

One day I awakened to an inner truth
I relinquished what was not mine
I did not hold anyone liable
I disowned my earthly possessions

Thence the day brightened
Everything seemed to fall in place
Each day brought a renewed excitement
Thence I was reborn to a new life

A perfect balance of past, present, and future

Physical things are important in the early phase of our lives as it gives us a sense of belonging. As one matures, there is a lesser value placed on things physical, and a new understanding of self and the inner being awakens. As one evolves there comes an understanding and comprehension beyond the spoken word. This phase of life when one is able to completely detach from physical attachment of material things is 'mukhti' an absolute detachment. This rebirth to a life of complete detachment is a balance of past, present, and future.

Preface to Takbir

The birth of my first child, born in Nairobi in the early seventies was a product of a difficult labor and loops of cord around the neck that had to be cut, resulting in significant neonatal asphyxia.

At the time of her birth I was a resident physician in pediatrics at the prestigious Kenyatta National Hospital in Nairobi, Kenya and the only other physician at hand in the obstetric birthing room.

Our child was born without vital signs, a fact that usually has alarming consequences because of a lack of oxygenation of the vital organs. While the OB-GYN doctor took care of my wife, I resuscitated our first child sucking the meconium, carrying out mouth to mouth resuscitation and gentle precordial thumb pressure. My attempts, but more likely a miracle brought her back to life.

My father was allowed visitation to recite a prayer in her ears at the neonatal unit and thereafter sat outside the unit reading the prayer book for twelve hours until day break without moving from his chair.

By morning our child was discharged from the neonatal unit to a regular bassinet as she was completely normal. My teacher and the chief of pediatrics, remarked that she was a miracle child. Indeed, she is our miracle child.

Our miracle child grew up into a magnificent young lady who graduated from Boston University with a combined degrees of a doctorate in jurisprudence and masters in international relation. The praise I believe is hers, as she decided not to leave us that day when she first arrived. As a physician, I am unable to explain her quick and miraculous recovery without deleterious effects of anoxia.

This poem is a dedication to the one responsible for the miracle. One that I have learned to understand and love as my savior.

Takbir

Your forefather's blood flows in your vein
Grandfather's *azan* may yet one day echo in your brain
Remember with reverence the path he walked
Forget not his bond and the language he talked

Loose not the link between you and them
In your days in life forget not His name
Allahu Akbar is His name
Learn to remember Him without shame

Forget not the family beacons of sharing
Remember His lessons of caring
Forget not the daily act of subjugation
Enjoy with solace His enunciation

The *azan* may someday echo in your brain
True as my blood flows in your vein
Forget not His name
Learn to accept Him without any shame

Takbir—Allahu Akbar literally means God is great

My poem "In Search of Truth" expresses my nonsectarian view of my maker

Preface to "Sage"

New Delhi 1970

Destiny is an uncharted territory
Mine was no different: a coincidental meeting with a young lady at a medical conference in New Delhi changed my destiny.

I was invited as a student participant to New Delhi to participate in an important conference. I was one of a group of nine students invited from all of India to offer my input on an inclusion of the "study of social sciences" in the Indian medical core curriculum. The nine students chosen had all demonstrated academic excellence in their respective medical schools. I was indeed lucky to be a part of such an elite group of students.

I was invited to assist with an introduction of a study of social sciences in the Indian medical school core curriculum-I had no knowledge that it would change my life's curriculum!

Sage

I fought the destiny that spelled your coming
The sage was right
You walked into my life, and my heart was soaring
I tried but in vain to lose your sight

He said a simple person with a simple heart
I will know the moment I see her face
I will try, but she will not part
I will show anger, but she will not lose grace

The sage told of many things that are now true
I disbelieved as my destiny was told
I have resigned to the picture of my life he drew
I fear not my departure now, as I grow old

Preface to "Guru"

My first and foremost Guru was my father who taught me much by living an exemplary life himself. He was a disciplined man who believed in a righteous, simple life. He inculcated in me the desire to follow the path of knowledge, caring and sharing. He spent most of his life teaching me valuable lessons, and now even after his passage in 1977, he is still my moral compass. My mother shared my father's work in grooming me to become an international citizen. She taught me cooking. She was the moderating influence in my life.

My next guru was a Brahmin teacher who took me to the Hindu temple to open my horizon to the Hindu philosophy in accordance with my father's wish. He told me of the epics of Mahabharata and Ramayana. He unknowingly prepared me for my future life with my wife. My next Guru was my high school physics teacher who taught me Vedic principles of health maintenance. He fostered a basis of a healthy mind in a healthy body.

During my first year of medical school in Poona at the B. J. Medical College I was a target of Hindu against Muslim violence. The medical students who inflicted much pain and harm were also my gurus as I learned first hand the pain of racial and ethnic hatred. They played an integral role in molding me into a secular humanitarian. They taught me to better understand the malice of a sectarian existence.

Countless others have contributed to who I am today.
Learning as I believe is from many sources but at the end of the day we have to acknowledge the gift and dignify the source.

The poem is a dedication to all my gurus

Guru

A salutation to all my teachers

Guru, how can I repay you for this knowledge?
Replied the guru; knowledge is like the flowing river
Drink its waters to your hearts content, but acknowledge
Only your participation makes you a deserving receiver

Like a ripple in the calm waters, each circle larger than the one before
Knowledge grows as the ripple moves distant from its source
The guru initiates this ripple and lets nature take its course
He is not aware of the student's future afore

Some students will drink the water and dignify its source
Some others will fail and take life with force
With the former, the guru rises to immortality
And with the latter he succumbs to fatality

True immortality is a perpetuation and growth of knowledge as knowledge transcends
all. It is the light that is lit forever.

Preface to "Charity"

Mother Teresa lived an exemplary life and showed the world that a human being has the inner strength to live a life of selfless giving. She was indeed a saint of our times.

Mahatma Gandhi and Martin Luther King have both taught us lessons of peaceful coexistence and Mother Teresa of Calcutta introduced an additional element of selfless giving.

This poem celebrates the work of this frail lady 'the little giant of Calcutta', who gave so much without a want of receiving.
She did not see color or creed. To her everyone was a child of God and deserved love and care.

Although she was of the Christian faith she embraced Vedic philosophy. This poem conceptualizes the Vedic philosophy of *atman*-the soul that is purified sequentially to its purest form the *paramatman*. Her life's dedication to India embraced the Vedic cultural attributes of selfless giving.

This poem is a dedication to the sister of charity, Mother Teresa

Charity

This poem was written in honor of Mother Teresa

True charity emanates from deep within our hearts
To give is not to part but to impart
This unique ability of sharing
Is not just a token but an expression of caring

The period between birth and death encompasses all
Life's relentless journey will rise and will fall
Give generously today that you may receive tomorrow
Give generously today that you may never need to receive tomorrow

Give not to glorify your being
True giving is without others hearing or seeing
Measure all giving not by the size of the gift
But the love that makes your soul uplift

Each incarnate passage of life an attempt to cleanse the *ataman*
A sequential purification to reach all that is pure—*paramatman*
Each of us will live a life of our own choosing
Each life an attempt to ascend without losing

Vedic theology—Atman is the soul and paramatman the most purified soul.

Preface to The Poem

America and the world were in denial of the genocide in Bosnia until the time mass graves were discovered in Bosnia, formerly a part of Yugoslavia.

When the news of the mass graves of Bosnia was broadcasted on the National Public Radio I was traveling from my office in Cambridge to my office in Brookline. The news was so overpowering that I was forced to pull over by the Charles River on my way, where I sat contemplating the news and the meaning of ethnic cleansing. While sitting by the river in my parked car I wrote the poem "Bosnia" on a Haveli restaurant's paper napkin.

The announcer was describing the discovery and the emotions of the living relatives of those buried in the mass graves who had amassed at the site. The announcer's apt description was heart-wrenching. The relatives remained *nameless* and those exhumed were *faceless*. The radio announcer expressed that the onlookers and those excavating did not know what to do with the remains excavated so they placed them in wood boxes for an appropriate disposal later. The forced starvation of these people and the mass killing scared our world once more. Whilst the atrocities went on unchecked the 'civilized world remained quiet'

The human race has not learned from its two world wars that both, incidentally saw its beginnings in Europe and that which brought about so much death and destruction of the human race.

As the genocide in Bosnia unfolded, the major powers failed to intervene in a timely manner to bring an end to it.

The United Nations remained dysfunctional and unable to react to the human suffering of these people just as it did in Rwanda and Sudan. We have failed to this day to recognize the original civilization of the Americas. The civilization that was nearly wiped out by the English and European invasion and immigration to the new world.

Our northern neighbor at least acknowledge them as the 'First Nation' while we in America still refer to them as Indian tribes!

We have to end genocide and human suffering in any shape or form.

Bosnia

An Ethnic Cleansing

A starving victim of European genocide

Nameless faces; Faceless bodies; Piles of bones
Some broken and some whole all piled in wood cases
How can I find my sister, my brother or my mother
How can I rest, when they have not

Mindless killing,
Senseless dealings,
Politicians inciting people to bear firearms,
Snatching innocent children from their mother's arms

What country, what patriotism can incite its people to kill
What is living without any will
No water to quench the thirst
Little food that one would not think of himself first

My heart is weeping with sorrow
I am fearful of the horrors of tomorrow
Walking skeletons deprived of food
Deprivation of human dignity does nobody any good

Preface to Mauthausen-Gusen

Genocide Photographed by Frank Shepard

Raphael Lambkin coined the word *genocide* which means a mass killing of the human race.

We are repeatedly told of the Nazi crimes but we have not learned restraint or compassion and the human race continues to commit genocide. The killing fields of Cambodia, the genocide in Iraq, the sacking of Palestine, the wanton killing of the Lebanese, the killings of the Hutus-Tutsis are just a few examples. We justify acts of war and support it by unholy political alliances. The genocide in the state of Gujarat is yet another untold and disguised story.

We have ventured into outer space and landed on the moon but we are bent on scarring mother earth with craters from our aerial bombing and the shock and awe attacks on civilizations that we choose to have philosophical, cultural and religious differences with.

The civilized world at this time is the biggest arms dealer, selling its killing machines to evolving nations. How can we demand abeyance from nuclear armament when we are the only nation that used nuclear weapons against humanity—not once but twice in succession and most likely a nation with the largest arsenal of nuclear weapons

I believe it's the right time for zero tolerance of nuclear armament bringing this world to a zero nuclear armaments program. No nation has the right to posses such catastrophic weapons, not now and not ever. Human race is not about a race for killing and possessing but a race of sharing and caring.

Mauthausen-Gusen

Austrian concentration camp

Piercing cries frozen in time
Unheard voices of victims silenced without any crime
Atrocities at Mauthhausen Gusen against man
A vivid testimonial of a race that had run insane

Flowers on tombs swaying in reverent silence
Protesting of past human sufferance
Chains and shackles anchored to the walls
Bitter memories of those captive within its halls

Rows of bunkers, remorseless tombs
Scores of bunk beds packed in its rooms
Gas chambers and incinerators, all exhibits of ghastly deeds
Surgery chambers designed to fulfill perverse Nazi needs

Mauthhausen town at the foot of this hill
Cannot wash off the stain left by this death-mill
Church steeples and townspeople trying to heal this scar
Left by their reluctance to spread the news of this atrocity afar

Humanity should never forget this gruesome act
Or fail to acknowledge it as a historic fact
Piercing cries frozen in time
Piercing cries must thaw to tell of this crime.

The poem was conceived the night of my visit to the historic concentration camp during
my visit to Austria as an invited guest of the Indian ambassador to Austria. The visit to
the camp deprived me of sleep for several nights following my visit to Mauthausen.

Dyer, The Butcher of Jallianwala Bhag

Reginald Edward Harry Dyer a son of a barman was a social misfit. At the age of 12 years he was removed from his parent's home. Eventually, he became a brigadier general of the British occupation forces in India.

On April 13, 1919, Indians gathered at the Jallianwala Bagh a public garden in Amritsar, the most sacred city for the Sikh Indians - for a nonviolent demonstration against the British occupation of India. It was a gathering of women, infants, children, and men. Three generations of families had gathered together to sing religious bhajans and listen to the voices of their elder's on the Rowlatt Act that was legislated to control "Quit India Movement."

Reginald Edward Harry Dyer marched his Forty-fifth Infantry Brigade to the gates of the garden with a machine-gun armored car capable of creating mayhem. The gates to the garden were too narrow for the passage of the machine gun armor car so he blocked the exit with the car and marched his infantry brigade into the garden. His men fired 1,650 bullet rounds into an unarmed gathering of women, children and men killing or maiming every standing person. Women threw their children into a well to protect them from Dyer's bullets and some others covered them with their own bodies to protect them from the bullets. The cry of death rang through the town deafening even the cries of the crows and bulbul.

Reginald Edward Harry Dyer should have hung by the gallows but he was discharged by the Hunter Committee for a mistaken notion of duty. The butcher of Amritsar, the architect of death returned back to his homeland, England to spend the remaining part of his life with his family and friends. He left behind in Amritsar orphaned children, widowed wives, childless mothers and fathers, and childless elders.

Genocide and massacres are not unique to Amritsar as history knows of similar massacres in Glencoe where a whole Scottish clan was massacred as they slept. The Zulu massacre during the Maji-maji uprising in South Africa, the Mau-Mau uprising of the Kikuyus of Kenya are just other examples of death and dying at the hands of an occupying force.

Gandhiji's question, "How long can a minority control a majority against its wishes" is still cogent in our generation where a minority occupying force is rejected by the majority of the populace.

Even today occupying forces commit atrocities against the innocent civilians in the name of the nation building. We are the victims of frequent sound bites on the air waves validating reasons for violating sovereignty of other nations, but our methods are still steeped in blood as was in Amritsar.

Jallianwala Bagh

Brig. Gen Reginald Dyer's Forty-fifth Infantry Brigade marched
Sound of army boots echoed off Jallianwala's walls thence parched
Within the walls twenty-thousand Indians gathered for a non-violent pact
To implement ways to repeal an unjust Rowlatt Act

British rifleman and two machinegun-armored cars blocked the garden
1,650 bullet rounds fired on the gathering without a warning or pardon
Ear shattering death cries and sight of the dying did not displease Dyer
That thirteenth of April, 1919, these men, women and children had no savior

Hunter Committee discharged Dyer's action as "a mistaken notion of duty"
He left India without equitable punishment or further scrutiny
Churchill and his British parliament rubber-stamped Hunter's proclamation
Thus the 'Butcher of Amritsar' returned to England without incarceration

In the quiet of each night the dead gather here to congregate
Cries of the dying are still heard as you enter its gate
The lit Flame of Liberty reminds us of the ghastly atrocity
Now Jallianvala a memorial for those massacred in Amritsar City

---

Rowlatt Act passed to legislate control of the Quit India Movement popularized by
Gandhiji and others

Preface to Missing in Action— A Broken Heart

Time and again our young men and women in uniform services put their lives at risk. How can a commander-in-chief send young men and women to their death without a moral justification?

Our men and women in uniform have been killed in Vietnam, and more recently in the Middle East without a significantly justifiable reason.

This poem is a salutation to these proud men and women who have put their lives at risk and also to the mothers and fathers who have felt the loss of their loved one.

Evolution of the Poem

As I was chatting with an elderly patient she broke into tears citing that she had forgotten that they had brought her the flag that day, a few years ago. Her son was missing in action. I was unable to comprehend her grief, and after much contemplation I awakened one night from deep sleep, at which time I wrote the poem that I presented her at a subsequent meeting.

She read the poem and cried requesting that I recite it for her. I did so, and she asked me if she may hug me, and humanity got the better of me. She cried on my shoulder talking of the long-lost son.

Her sadness told me of the true meaning of *"missing in action."*

Missing in Action

Eyes searching the horizon
For her long lost son gone without reason
MIA, what does that really mean,
Ask the mother whose son she has not seen

Young in age at nineteen
Ready to serve his country with very high esteem
No questions asked at the time
Now lost much before his prime

No salute or folded flag brings back the son
The mother questions what the country has done
Did his life or death win peace or the war?
Ask the mother whose heart it tore

Preface to Ground Zero

In 1964 about the time I was admitted to a medical school I believed that racial discrimination in an highly advanced civilization such as the United States was an improbability. However at about that time in Mississippi two black men Eddie Moore and Henry Hezekiah were beaten by some white thugs and drowned to death that year in 1964.

The ethnic Americans are a forgotten nation in their own country. Similarly, the natives of Australia and New Zealand have lost their country to an immigrant population. Until recently in South Africa and Rhodesia, color segregation was accepted by the "civilized" world.

Disproportionate numbers of African Americans are incarcerated even now, some for very insignificant offense. The nation that promoted and later abolished slavery is struggling to bring about integration and assimilation of its people.

A dark Dominican physician friend returning home after anesthetizing a surgical patient at a local hospital in Boston was stopped, strip searched and the contents of his car were thrown by the roadside by a police officer. His crime, DWB—driving while black!

We elected an African American president through a transparent and democratic process to lead our free nation but some still question his American heritage.

Birth of the Poem

I was invited to recite a poem at the famous Mechanic's Hall in Worcester at a Solidarity Meeting, a few days following the 9/11 Twin Tower tragedy.

After the 9/11 tragedy an American Sikh was tortured to death and an Indian student hog tied and cigarette burnt by some white boys who later carried him in the trunk of his pizza delivery car to be dumped in a nearby river. Fortunately he was saved.

Most believe in social integration and color acceptance but there is jingoism still prevalent in some sections of our civilized society.

My poem grieves our loss and prompts tolerance and self-examination.

Ground Zero: A Tribute

Oh, sweet Twin Towers from your fire let rise the Phoenix of love
Love that knows not color
For what color is the pain we feel?
Is it white? Is it black? Or is it brown?

Wrath and anger only begets more anger
And wanton killing only add numbers of those already dead
Is it not love that triumphs over all evil?
And is it not love that begets more love?

Sadly, we lost our brothers and sisters that day
We lost a father, a child and our only love
Did we not lose much, not to learn to build our future with bricks of love?
Did we not learn to rebuild with the mortar of caring and sharing?

What color is our pain?
Is it white or is it black or is it brown?
If truly our pain knows not color, why target those with color?
Why then burn their shop, their house, or their place of worship?

Throw not bricks of hate into their homes
Hate them not for the color of their skin
They are as much Americans, just like the rest of us
And their pain is no less, as in that rubble lie their sons and daughters

What color is our pain?
Is it white or is it black or is it brown?
Just as our pain knows not color
Let our love also be color blind

Preface to Mr. President—
Modern Day Genocide

A past president of the United States of America ordered an invasion of the sovereign nation of Iraq with prefabricated and intentional lies that Iraq housed weapons of mass destruction "WMBD." He put our armed forces at risk for dubious reasons and personal miscalculations. His chief of staff told the world on national television of the location of weapons of mass destruction which later on was proven wrong or labeled as misguided intelligence.

We have by our actions made a nation cripple. An article in the British medical journal, *Lancet**, Oct. 11 2006 reported horrendous numbers of Iraqi civilians that died since the invasion.

Who must accept the moral responsibility for this genocide?

---

www. thelancet.com published Oct. 11, 2006 DOI: 10. 1016/S 0140-6736 (06) 69491-9

Mr. President

Mr. President, I choose to sit in silence
Not that I am dazzled by your brilliance
Weapons of mass destruction you sought
You destroyed the cradle of humanity* and found it not

Was it a common greed and desire for fossil oil?
Was that the only reason for your unwarranted armed recoil?
When you talk of that country's potential for nuclear action
Forget not the nation that caused Hiroshima's destruction

If democracy is the will of the people
We the people truly did not wish a nation cripple
In full army regalia your general announces
Christian God is far superior he pronounces

Is this a quest for democracy?
Or just another holy crusade shrouded in secrecy?
We preach thou shall not kill and we kill
We preach thou shall not steal and we steal

Mr. President I choose to sit in silence
Not that I am dazzled by your brilliance
Your actions have made this world an unsafe place
I pray in silence for forgiveness and our maker's grace

Many such men before you have come and gone
Death and destruction in their lives they have sown
Mr. President I prefer to pray in silence
Fervently pleading our maker's forgiveness for our penance

Garden of Eden at the delta of the Tigris-Euphrates

Preface to What Reason for War— Troubled Conscience

An end to the American invasion of Vietnam came about mainly because of frequent civilian demonstrations against the Vietnam War which awakened the conscience of our nation (Thank you flower children).

We share vivid memories of the remains of the American soldiers brought back to the country during our invasion of Vietnam.

During our invasion of Iraq and Afghanistan our dead soldiers were brought back in great secrecy. True information of dead soldiers trickled very slowly, as did the recent mistreatment of veterans at the Walter Reed Army Hospital and our failure to recognize post traumatic stress syndrome.

The country was not aware of the true numbers of the Armed Forces disabled due to head injuries until the time some of these soldiers broke rank to tell their story.

This poem is dedicated to mothers whose troubled conscience has forced them to camp outside the White House and also organize protests.

What Reason for War?

Countless innocent lives lost in war
Sifting through lists of names until fingers run sore
These names represent only our children lost
What of the children of the country we occupy or host?

What country what patriotism sends its children to war?
Ask those grieving mothers whose hearts it tore
Private Abraham, Ram, DeJesus, Mohamed, who were they? we ask
Now silenced by war they speak not of their morbid task

Take to the street mother and bring your children home
Demand of the country to return back your lives to norm
Leaders in Washington care only of their false personal pride
Deaf to the mothers who only ask for truth and justice they side

Day after day our dead soldiers repatriate back in ceremonious casket
Their worldly belongings presented in a tri-colored basket
Mother speak up for the life of your child whilst he is still living
End this carnage for a life of love, sharing, caring and giving

Preface to Urban Jungle

I was born in East Africa and came to the United States in 1975 on a Fellowship to a Harvard Hospital. At the time of my arrival to Boston there was much outrage as children from the inner city were bused to various schools to bring about equality in our education system.

During that time I was mugged at a knifepoint just outside my apartment in the parking lot on Saint Alfonso Street in near proximity to Boston's old Mission Hill project. My assailants could not remove my wedding band and were planning to cut my finger and may have done so if some vehicles had not arrived in the parking lot. I was lucky as they got away with only my wallet which contained two dollars and my Rado watch, an anniversary gift from my wife.

Africa has frequently been described as the Dark Continent and only after my arrival to the United States I realized that the urban jungle was worse than the jungles of Africa.

We hear of the inner city shootings almost daily. These shootings are mostly attributed to gang violence and drug wars. During my residency I saw my fair share of gunshot victims brought to the emergency room. That is where I learned first hand that John Doe was not a real name!

In the jungle you are only hunted for food but in the urban jungle the reason may be dubious.

The Urban Jungle

The sound of gun fire awakened our gentle neighbor
His only child lay in a pool of blood breathing with much labor
Shadowy figures moved away in the veil of the night
Dark and faceless they quickly moved out of sight

They say his son witnessed a killing on his way to his school
Now he lay lifeless soaked in a crimson pool
Man, the most vicious predator
No respect for his own species or his creator

Sobbing aloud the father questioned of his God
Why his race chose this evil road
He believed that man was created in His own image
Then why this need for such wanton carnage

Preface to The Heartless Hunter—
My Passive Participation

I had repaired a very badly disrupted shoulder of a patient who approximately three or four years later walked into my office to give me the great news that his shoulder was working well.

He requested a medical fitness certification for an application for a compound bow license to remain in force for a two-year renewal.

He stated that he hunted deer—with his compound bow. I was unable to issue the certification as his shoulder had not returned back to normal and I was concerned that the rigor of his stated activity would likely damage his shoulder.

This poem is written with the heartless hunter in mind who kills not for hunger but for pleasure.

The Heartless Hunter

The string twanged as the arrow left the bow
With eerie accuracy found the heart of the grazing doe
Blood gushed and the doe fell to its knee
Twitching it lay in a crimson bloody sea

The hunter rejoiced at his sure kill
Slid down the tree and ran to the doe down the hill
He did not kill for hunger
The sight of blood brought no remorse or anger

Man the most vicious predator
Little or no respect for his own creator
Life without much reason for living
How can humanity condone such killing?

Preface to Next Five Poems

Organized religion has made God a proprietary right. Some among us still believe that they are the chosen people! Others believe that the right to heaven can only be granted to their followers.

When the white settlers came to Africa they converted the "nonbelieving heathens" to worship their God with an enticement for heaven and gifts. Only later did the human race find that the *Homo Erectus* originated in Africa thereby making the Africans the earliest known civilization to walk the earth.

Pursuit of God should be through acts of kindness, excellence of morality, simple existence and love for fellow human beings and all God's creations. Why is it incumbent for us to embrace an organized religion?

Akbar the great Moghul king married a Hindu Rajput princess and proposed *'Din-i-Ilahi'*, the religion of the masses that incorporated good of all Indian religions—an exciting religion based on conscience and morality that emphasized a true sense of humanity.

Every child needs to grow in a house of sharing and caring, where no child is less, where color has no meaning and where there is a religion that emphasizes the highest standards of morality.

He Is Who He Is

Words echoing, a thousand sounds
His name resonating in the dome
Bouncing off the geometric walls
Boomeranging back to the disciple's ears

His name engraved in blue jade
Walls shimmering in the dim evening light
Call for prayers resounding in the hall
The believer's brow fused to his prayer mat

Bliss yet unknown to some
To others His light an eternal glow
His name dispelling fright and fear
Who is He that lives within him?

Say His name not in vain
He who is the Giver
He who is the embodiment of truth
To the believer He is his maker

Allah, God, Prabhu, Mungu, Jahova, Ishwar

We Call Him by Many Names

I have traveled far and wide, stopping from place to place
I have knocked on so many doors just to seek your face
I have awakened from deep sleep, gazing in the dark of the night
I have pursued this path just to have you in my sight

Bronzed from base metal to all that is pure
Each life in search of knowledge that is sure
Desire for virtue has beckoned me to your light
I pray that you always keep me in your sight

I have heard your name spoken in rhyme and song
I have responded to the sound of your disciple's gong
I have held my brow to the bosom of the earth
I have subjugated to you in life and each rebirth

The sage speaks that you hold the reins of life
You protect all from misery and strife
I have heard your name in many tongues
I have sung your song with every breath of my lungs

I remember not that I have seen you yet
In my time of need was it you that I met?
When all was lost and nowhere to go
Was it you who delivered me from my foe?

God has become a proprietary right. My God is superior to all the rest, some say.
Even with gods we discriminate.
Why can we not say a silent prayer in any tongue as in a Bahai Temple? Does God
only understand Sanskrit, Arabic, Latin or Aramaic? Does he not understand the
universal language of love, sharing and caring?
The next three poems express my veiws of my maker

Believer

Many faces of truth make our world

If there exists a disbelief in your word
How can there be a belief beyond your word
Mistrust must embody all such disbeliefs
Disbelief in your word propagates mistrust

Truth has many faces
You may prefer to accept God in your heart
Temple congregates may deprecate your absence
To those your absence is an expression of a non-acceptance

God must know those that just guild the tower of worship
And also those who are true believers
To some God only exists in their belief
To the atheist His existence is not relevant

The atheist may be kind, generous and all-giving
To the fanatic the atheist is Godless, with no place in heaven
But what of his kindness, generosity and gentle nature
God must recognize his selfless deeds

God recognizes all faces
A face of the one in the house of worship
A face of the one who worships Him privately
A face of the one who worships Him with his kind deeds

Where Does He Reside

One who has not introspected finds faults with others
Fighting the devil, not vacating the devil residing within
Searching for God in places of worship
Walking the desert sands in search of God

Sanyas deep in the jungles
He knows not that God is in the soul not touched with greed
God is in the soul that knows not to hurt
God is in the innocence of a child

God is in the jungle animal who knows no malice
Cage it only to make it loose its soul
In His eyes there are no masters and no slaves
All are equal in His eyes

In Search of Truth

Life spent in search of truth
Searched where it was not
Searched amongst the poorest of the poor
Searched amongst the richest of the rich

It was not that they lacked the truth
But that I lacked the wisdom to see it
A man deprived of sight, searching for the light outside
When all the time the light was present within

Now awakened to this wisdom I see the truth
The sight that sees not outside but within
I searched for my god in temples, churches and masjids
And I found him not

I looked for my God without
When all the time he lived within
True belief is in the depth of our inner most thoughts
And not within the walls of the temples, churches and masjids

For these walls may be destroyed by nature or by force
But how can anyone destroy an idea that has no shape or form?
That idea that is a constellation of all thoughts pure
My God resides in the realms of this inner truth

Fears of the Night

As night creeps in, hidden fears awaken
That what did not exist in daylight now exists
Body in deep sleep but the mind racing
Muscles tense, twitching and cramping

Rapid eye movement, deep sleep all names of sleep
Crescendo of fear
Heart racing as in flight or fright
Tossing and turning and mumbling incoherently

Premonition of what is to come
Fears of past encounters revisited
An inner alarm alerting of future encounters
Primordial animal instinct awakened in the subconscious

Life's Learning Experience

Life's learning experience where does it begin, where does it end?
His emissary laden with knowledge when and where will he send?
Wisdom gathered in each life must perpetuate hereafter
The journey begins here but must continue much after

Soul wizened with passage in each life
Each rebirth earning a right of passage without strife
Deaf ears refusing to hear His call
Likely destined to return once more to purify their soul

Bliss of heaven is the right of every pure soul
Subjugation alone will not grant a passage to His hall
Love, kindness and respect for all things living
The path is uncovered only with such kind deeds of giving

Believe not that He resides only in designated places
He is omnipresent and has many faces
His being is surrounded by an eternal light
Learn to know Him in your heart and not by your sight

Fear of the Occult

Birthstones, crosses, incense, sage weed, lavender, candles and *diyas*
Chanting prayers and performing séance
Futile attempts to understand the occult
That which does not exist is alive only in darkness

Tarot cards, *vastu shastra*, *feng shui*, all attempts to align the stars
Sacrifices on dark, moonless nights
Thresholds painted in blood to ward off evil
Fear only exists in the heart of the sinner

The pure soul focuses on the path of the righteous
He holds His book of laws in his heart
He does not worry of what the world thinks of him
He only follows His commandments

The Cycle of Life

Would my knowledge of today have changed my yesterday?
What I know today I did not know yesterday
My yesterday was fueled by love and a sense of duty
My knowledge of today may help shape my tomorrow

I learned from my mistakes
I learned from my mentor's wisdom
I cannot know everything there is
Humility is a virtue that opened doors of knowledge

I have learned to respect my elders
My teachers are my source and guidance
I continue to learn from many sources
My life is a journey of boundless learning

Each day I wake up to a new day of learning
I edify my teachers, parents and elders
They stumbled so that I may not
Their karma must be my nirvana someday

Today's knowledge cannot change my yesterday
But it will guide me to my tomorrow
My expectations will be tempered
My past shaped my present to improve my tomorrow

My past, a memory of bygone days
My present, a bonus of my past
My future, a vision of my tomorrow
Tomorrow, where yesterday and today confluence

Knock on Your Door

If you hear a knock on your door but find no one
Look not with your eyes but your heart
Thence you may see what is not visible
Rejoice that you are loved

When you have a hiccup or your eye twitches
Know that you are remembered
The whistling wind carries my voice
Hear it not with your ears but your heart

When I am not there I am there in your thoughts
When I am with you I leave my impression in your mind
I may be gone but in your mind's eye I live on
If you hear a knock on the door rejoice that you are loved

Miracle of Daybreak

Fragrant gentle breeze of fresh blossoms
Morning rays awakening all life
Cacophony of chirping birds searching food
Squirrels bouncing from branch to branch in playful frolic

Occasional honking of the Canada geese flying overhead
Flapping wings of two ducks landing in my pool
Distant sound of car-engine coming to life
Thud of the newspaper landing on my driveway

House lights coming on as its occupants awaken
Barking of the dog on his morning walk
Smell of freshly brewed coffee
Sound of the shower in an adjacent room

Morning sounds that we all know so well
Yet we rarely remember to acknowledge
Life's diurnal cycle of sleeping and awakening
Are just ordinary pleasures of an extraordinary life

A Thunderstorm of a Weeping Soul

The sky thundered and lightning broke through
Rain poured, bringing an end to the drought
Legend has it that the sky weeps
When a kind soul is hurt

Rainwater meandered to join its brethren
Together they strengthened, removing all obstacles in its flow
First the leaves and debris and then cars and all things loose
Thunder clapped and more water flowed

Lightning struck again and again inviting total darkness
All things alive moved to ground higher than its flow
It poured as the kind soul wept in silent sobs
Only his maker knew his pain, unleashing his wrath in response

He silently prayed to the god of his ancestors
The same god that guided him to do his bidding
He prayed as water swept by his feet and rose to his face
He struggled to breathe but mumbled on

As the chest heaved no more and his breath froze
Lightning cracked tearing the sky into jagged pieces
Quiet followed, the rain stopped and the waters ebbed
All scurried back down from their perches, all except one

Thence the kind soul lived no more

Maturity

Each step unfolding its own story
A man who has achieved fame and glory
Voice mature with years of phonation
String of words in precise expression

Facial creases and gentle gestures
All telling of a multitude of past adventures
Spring and fall past and gone
But winter leaves not just skin and bone

Gentle snowflakes melting on the silver gray hair
Dripping down the furrows of his face
Brown eyes expressive of life that has been fair
High spirit and gentle grace

Each season leaving its mark
Not affecting the soft interior beneath the seasoned bark

A Promise

Amaajee our mother

Amaajee, we have enjoyed your shade for many years
Now that you have left us we are truly lost
Our strength we believe must come from your teaching
We promise to live our lives by example just as you did yours

We will share our joy and good fortune with others
And we will share the pain and sorrow of our family and friends
You have left us, Amaajee
But your light will continue to shine through our progeny and us

We will celebrate your life and not grieve
We will smile even though our hearts are sad with your parting
We will continue your legacy of gentle loving
We will continue to win the invincible and strive to be better beings

Until we meet again

A parting tribute to a mother

The Fruit Tree

The fruit tree stood its ground against raging winds and rain
Holding its boughs close not succumbing to the strain
In drought the earth cracked and parched
But the tree sent its roots deep down until water it searched

In early spring covered with sweet-smelling flowers
Enticing bees and birds with its fragrant clovers
Offering its nectar in favor for its fruit to bear
Passing travelers eating its fruit and carrying some to share

Now that the fruit is gone the tree is forgotten
The bark is cracked and the roots rotten
Does anyone remember the tree that bore sweet fruit?
The tree that fought violent winds and rain with its entire brute

Lord of Death and Life

With open arms I await to offer my last breath to thee
You are so very well-known to me
That day when the lady dying of cancer took her last sigh
I felt your presence as you passed me by

Desperately resuscitating my own child I saw you then
I saw you smile and I felt your Zen
I knew not before that time that you could also gift life
I knew you only as the Lord of death and strife

You revealed yourself again as my mother gasped for air
I fought you with all the courage I could dare
Once again you gifted me my mother's life
I acknowledge your deed, O Lord of death and strife

With open arms I now welcome thee
You have always been fair to me
Now that I know you also posses the power to give life
I salute thee, O Lord of death and strife

This poem is dedicated to an eminent physician, a true friend and a magnanimous being, my good friend Jayant Khettry who left us much before his time.

Digger of the Well

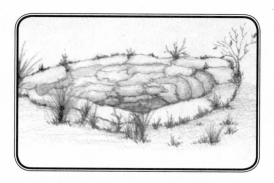

Each day spent toiling to dig the well deeper
Each evening returned to the top without a sight of water
Then the water seeped just as he doubted the well would yield
And to its brim with cool, sweet water it filled

Its water soothe the thirst of many who traveled this land
Resting weary feet from days of travel over the burning sand
Each day the digger kept the well in good repair
Talking of it with the fondness of his own heir

Now that the digger is old skin and bones
He is unable to repair or carry more heavy stones
The wall is crumbling from need of work
He pleads for help but the travelers call him an old jerk

He searches the horizon wishing for his child to return
Tearless eyes are now so dry they only burn
The well is still filled with water to its brim
But the wall is crumbling like him, who was once fit and trim

The Evening Song

Young lovers responding to gentle, teasing touch
Sleepy eyes quietly saying so much
Pounding heart fluttering, like a caged blue jay
Lovers bewitched by the melody of the sun's fleeting ray

Day yielding with reluctance to the dark of the night
All day critters preparing to retreat safely out of sight
The meetinghouse bells announcing the evening prayer
Disciples deep in prayer to their nameless savior

One more glorious day passed without a care
Day's earnings to have hold, and partly share
Bedded for one more restful night
Until awakened by the first ray of light

Winter Solstice

This winter's day is the most unusual day
Morning breeze freshened my face as I sat to pray
Each life past, present and future fused into one
Salutation to work that yet remains to be done

This winter's day is a most unusual day
My heart's wish took birth today they say
Each life and each rebirth in your company spent
Reborn in each life just for you I am sent

I may be far but you will always remain near
Separation may test our resolve my dear
This winter's day is the most unusual day
May this morning breeze renew your hope I pray

Dedicated to my child, very far but very close

Architects of Destruction

Man occupies the land where the lion roamed
Lynx, mink and fox have a bounty on their head
Even the tiger's skin adorns his parlor
Man's superior intelligence destroyed his kingdom

Man must learn of the ecological balance as his salvation
The bats eat the mosquito that spreads malaria
The crow scavenges the carcass of the dead to the bone
The wolf weeds out the sick caribou preventing sickness in the herd

Without the bee there is no pollination
Without pollination there is no fruit
Without trees there is soil erosion and sink hole
We are pumping out the fossil oil from the bowel of the earth

Are we removing the hydraulic fluid that may prevent imploding
He who made us must have a sense of equilibrium
Coexistence is good for humanity
Human race must check its exponential growth

Scarcity of food, clean air, and water is not far
Leasing land in countries outside is now a routine
We are sucking the mother earth dry
Our solution may lie in understanding nature

Coexistence with all life forms
Incas and the Pharaohs perished leaving little trace
Will it take another tsunami to clean our slate
Must Noah build yet another raft to prevent extinction

Ahimsa

So many walked through the doorway
None noticed the little creature writhing in pain
Vomiting blood incessantly
Is he not God's creation too, he wonders

Who poisoned him and why
Why is he less than the one who set his trap
Did he not deserve a right of coexistence
Who gave man a right to kill

A mouse whose family is awaiting his return
Who will now protect his progeny
Who will warn them of the human danger
Are they all destined to a similar end

So many walked the doorway
Who thought of him as God's creation
Noah carried his kind to safety
Did God give man a right to kill?

Ahimsa Sanskrit word—to not injure

Nelson Mandela

The sun set in South Africa today
The Son of Africa can never set
The Son of Africa may rise no more
But Madiba shall live in our hearts for eons to come

A gentle giant that walked the steps of Gandhi
A man transformed from a militant to a humanitarian
The sun of Africa may have set
But this Son of Africa will never set

Gandhi, Mandela, King share a common path
A path of love for God and nonviolence
A path of forgiveness, and kindness
In our heart these sons of humanity remain immortal

The Son of Africa has arisen once again

Final Journey

Lying lifeless, soaked in my own excreta
My father's lifeline all lost with me
My children know not even my rites of interment
They have learnt not the prayers for the dead

Fragrance of flowers surround me that I smell not
Friends and family gathered for a final good-bye
Exalting my virtues now that I lie dead
In life they overlooked even my simplest need

I lie in this grave supine when on my side I must be
Not washed with soap and rubbed with camphor
But drenched in perfumes that mute the stench
Where is my shroud I ask, did I deserve it not?

My veins pumped with mortician's poisons
My hair plastered down with a sordid gel
My orifices not with sandalwood swabs
My face painted unnaturally as if alive

In life they knew not of my simple need
I stood in life alone as on my prayer mat
I looked to the right and I found them not
I looked to the left and I found them not

I now walk this path alone toward the eternal light
I am beckoned by my mother's voice
I see them all who have come to carry me home
I have not a need now, as I am home

Ghost in the Attic-Dhari

Mombasa is a wonderful coastal town in Kenya on the shores of the Indian Ocean. The weather is balmy and the Kiswahili people very friendly. I was born in Mombasa at Kullsum Masi, my maternal aunt's house whom I referred to as my second mother and referred to her as Kullsum Mama.

Mombasa is where my mother was born too, so it was natural for me to spend my school vacations in Mombasa. My mum's oldest sister was a disciplinarian with a heart of gold. I loved her and all my maternal aunts very much. I miss my summer days spent in Mombasa.

As a routine when in Mombasa I lived with Kullsum Mama, but once in a while my great aunt stole me away to her house. The family home that belonged to all the four sisters was an old home that scaled four floors. My great aunt occupied the third floor and the top of the house that was a sun room that we called the Dhari. I loved to sleep in the Dhari as it was the highest point in the house and the glass wall gave it a wonderful ambiance.

On one such day that I was with my great aunt I was offered the most sought after room, the Dhari. As I was sleeping in the Dhari I had an uncanny experience that I was not able to comprehend. My bed shook and rocked as I slept. I hung my belt on the metal frame of the bed, and its buckle hit the metal frame, making musical sounds. When I awakened in the morning I told my Great aunt of the experience and she casually mentioned, "He means no harm, he was just being playful."

I later found out from my cousins that there was a presence felt and sometimes an Arab Sheikh was seen in the house. There seemed a peaceful coexistence and the children joked of his presence, but I refused to sleep in the Dhari at least not until I was a teenager!

Ghost in the Attic

Sat alone in the room
Highest point of the house
Knew not of ghosts
Ghosts knew not of me

The bed shuddered a little at first
Then shook like a leaf in a strong breeze
Not understanding the reason
Believed the house shook with the wind

Morning rays stopped the shaking
Though the wind continued to howl
At breakfast I mentioned the shaking
My aunt assured me he will harm me not

Divergent Path

Divergent path away from home
Winds of time erased your foot prints
Perched on your father's shoulder when little
Now gone but the weight of parting I must shoulder

Gone to a place and time unknown to me
Far from an identity I dreamed of you
I knew my heart beat was once yours
Now my heart does not even know of its own beat

Your pain I feel as my own
My parents' hopes of me shattered
Their identity lost by my own divergent path
My hope now lives only in my dreams

When I part my identity will pass on with me
Nothing to show to those that went before me
Just scars left of choices made
Stooped now not with age but the weight I carry

Giving Thanks

This one day that we exalt relationships
A sacrificial bird its center piece
Remaining three hundred and sixty-four days of disregard
One isolated patch on bygone days

Thanks giving?
An oxymoron
Receiving without true giving
Society of limitless wants

The sacrificial bird cannot heal
Scars of three hundred and sixty-four days of neglect and abuse
Father died without a goodbye, mother left in a nursing home
Spending days in misery awaiting an end

Adieu, Our Friend and Colleague

A chance to know you better now remains in vain
We grieve our loss that you have passed on
We know not of your rite of passage
A rite of passage we may not comprehend

Life's journey where does it begin and where does it end?
Earthly wisdom may have earned you a rite of passage
Or maybe your need away outweighed your need amongst us
Something that we mortals may not comprehend

Remember us in your new abode
As we remember you here on earth
When our time is right, greet us with your endearing smile
Adieu, our friend and colleague until we meet again

I wrote this poem as a tribute to a colleague that passed on

God

What you seek you will find it not
You seek too hard to find it
Enter deep within yourself
You may thence be enlightened

Master your innermost self
Not your friends or foe
Power is not in the might
But in the sublime that deflects it

Air, water and fire are your friends
Elements enraged may cause devastation
Tame the beast
Let the elements be your friends

Do not look for God where you will find him not
He is where you may least expect
He is with the mother who grieves
He is with the orphan seeking mother's love

God is in the hungry on the curbside
He is in the bird fallen from its nest
He is not in the four walls of the Temple
He is a free spirit that cannot be locked in four walls

Breath in deeply as He is in the air you breathe
Pollute not His ale, water is life
Enjoy the warmth of His fire as it is His gift
Respect fire, water and air as God flows from the elements to you

Loss of a Loved One

In your arms I touched the heavens
Your touch brought me bliss and joy
Now you are gone and I know my loss
Sorry, I hesitated to acknowledge your love

I hear you in the dead of the night
When it is dark I sense your light
I feel your presence as I sleep
Your fragrance lingers in my life

The wind whispers your words
Rustling leaves remind me of you
I awaken to the creaking of the door
Only to be aware that you are gone

My loss so early in life
How am I to console myself
Life without you cannot be life
Adieu until we meet again

I lost my parents some years ago. Both passed on early in life. They did a lot for me and I was not able to return their love and well being as I was struggling with a grueling medical residency and the responsibility of a young family.

I return their kindness in my daily life.

I Am Who I Am

I am who I am
I am made up of many parts
Parts of me I cannot claim mine
But a gift of inheritance of eons

I am known by my father's name
My mother carried me in her womb
I am who I am
One whole made of many parts

Alchemy of many parts
I am who I am
Some from my father
And some from my mother

I am who I am
Part father and part mother
Part that I blended as I matured
Who am I then

My father's son
Or my mother's son
What of mine genetic inheritance
I am who I am parts of many parts

Preface to Life: A Paradox

My values were somewhat askew, and not unlike most first generation immigrants, I found a need to prove myself worthy of the privilege of being a part of this great democracy. Later in life I started visualizing an imbalance in my life. I had valued material things even though culturally and rooted in my heritage such want was deprecated. I refer to my earlier days as, *"identity crisis."* I found a need to prove my worth. The driving force was not without its merits as it made me excel in my professional life and helped me to establish a firm foundation for my young family. It allowed me to afford tangible and necessary things, such as a great education for my two children, who both went to excellent private schools in Boston and later great colleges. I am fortunate that my children did not throw away the opportunity and excelled in education to enter worthy professions-an achievement that is the crowning of my efforts as a first generation Indian American with roots in East Africa.

In my fifties or just before that I shifted the gears of my thought process. I distinctly remember my fiftieth birthday celebration, which my wife and children wanted to celebrate in a big way. I thought of it and requested to celebrate my birthday as a fund raiser for charity. I was fortunate as my friends and family respected my wish, and we raised just a little more than twenty thousand dollars. A good friend not only wrote out a check for charity but also presented me with a classic Mountblanc ball-point pen, that I accepted but I wrote a personal check to the charity for an amount just a little more than the cost of the fine writing instrument. I used the pen with much pride and joy, and unlike most of my pens it served me well for about ten years. I remember I inadvertently left the pen on a bench at one of the hospital operating changing room, at a time when articles were disappearing but I found the pen on the bench on my return.

I cherished the pen and I decided to give it to my son who had completed his medical training. I know that he cherishes the gift just as much. Over time I have enjoyed the experience of random giving, hoping to disown every material thing that I value, much before my time, and enjoy the joy of giving in my lifetime.

Life: A Paradox

When I had not, I had it all
When I had it all, I had not
Life is a roller-coaster ride
I am seemingly still, but life is zooming by

What we have, we value not
What we have not, we value
Life is a paradox
A pursuit of what we have not

With our eyes we see not
What the blind perceive we see not
What can there be to see if our heart feels not
When the heart feels not, what value of sight

Democracy of Fools

In the company of fools
Fools know not, what they know not
Fools innocuous of wisdom
Wise men innocuous of the fools

Democracy of the fools
Whereby fools rule
Wise men herded and used
Wisdom of no value in the democracy of fools

Fools out vote the wise by sheer numbers
Wise labor hard to feed the fools
Fools benefit from industry of the wise
Common wealth of the wise for the fools

Interdependence

As I first stood up to walk my parents held my hand
As I walked waddling at best they walked by my side
As I walked to school they worried but let go
As I returned they waited to hear of my adventures

As I sought independence my teachers held my hand
As I faltered they gently brought me back on track
As I learned more they taught me even more
As I left the school they wished me well

As I grew up my friends held my hand
As I worried they lessened my load
As I walked ahead they walked behind
As I accomplished they celebrated my success

As I had my children my family held my hand
As I marched on they spelled my future
As I worried they rallied to my support
As I matured they shared my wisdom

Life is all about interdependence

Sweet Bitterness

Those who praised me flocked my abode
My favorite teacher who praised me
Those critical of me I kept away
Away from me those critical of me

I have learned thence not from praises
But from my critics who saw through my façade
I stand tall now and not weak
Strong from weathering criticism

Life has taught me to learn from the learned
Wisdom comes not from the weak
Learning is not from those that toe my line
But from those that do not slacken the line

Life's Journey

Driving life's journey
Sometimes swerving to the right
Sometimes swerving to the left
Believing to be in control, yet completely out of control

Feeling of control espousing a false sense of security
Feeling out of control froth with disdain and failure
Let Him be the driver of your journey
Move into the back seat and enjoy the ride

Relax, breathe His air, and enjoy His creations
When He swerves to the right or left
It is to remind you that He has taken charge
Close your eyes and think of Him for eternal peace

For every bump let Him know He is driving
He responds to words in every language
Believe not that He only understands ancient languages
His divinity transcends all languages even a gesture is enough

Remind Him of your needs and desires
He will detour just to save you and all near you
In time you will be one with Him
Thence your journey will truly begin

Mine Shroud

Mine shroud fenestrated with holes
Many left by people unknown
Most others by those near and dear
Body covered yet mostly bare

As I lived a life of truth
Some stood hidden daggers drawn
I knew not of my enemies
But friends I trusted

Now they flock around me
Tears in their eyes
Some still with daggers drawn
Weary that I may resurrect

Life's Labor Lost

Each day spent in toil
Each night returning home with the bounty of the soil
Too late to awaken his son and daughter
Too late to hear their song and laughter

Each day spent in toil
Each night returning home with bounty of the soil
Toiled for their education, shelter, and food
Worked hard to provide his home with all that was good

Each night their mother told him that his word was spoken
And each day she assured him that his story was written
Each night he slept with a belief that his efforts were not spent in vain
Each hour and each day he spent never for his own personal gain

Now much older and wiser he has read the story that she had written
And aware of the words that were spoken
Only to realize that whilst he worked, his children knew not of him
But of his wife and knew nothing of his life's theme

The story written was not of his work or deeds
But of their mother who fulfilled all their needs
But still each day he continues to toil
And each night he returns with the bounty of the soil

A father in our society is a forgotten entity as he is away from home attempting to earn the daily bread. Some such as me are fortunate to be a dual-working family, where both parents share equally the duties of parenting and financial upkeep of the family. I know of one such friend who missed to realize the need for equilibrium until too late in life.

Protoplasmic Pain

Have you felt your blood boil in your veins?
Painfully bubbling incessantly
Pretend not, to know my pain
When pain you have felt not

Drowning in my own tears
Tears that ran inside flooding my chest
Pretend not, to know pain
When pain you have felt not

Have you gazed deep in the silent night?
Only to hear your heart sob
Pretend not, to know pain
When pain you have felt not

Have you felt each cell in your body grieve?
Until no cell is left without pain
Pretend not, to know pain
When pain you have felt not

I felt that pain when I lost my own
I felt it as I carried the lifeless body
I felt it as I covered it with earth
I felt it then and now as I live in my grief

Pierce the Shroud of the Night

Throw your stone skywards to pierce the shroud of the night
Know your inner strength and might
Even on darkest night the shroud has star-holes of light
Each hole from a stone that pierced the shroud of the night

Judge not your strength by your sinews but by your mind
Mind that has the power of a different kind
Power that can awaken sleeping destinies of hearts to be reborn
Power that reshapes sick nations now tattered and torn

Those enlightened know the path of the truth
Path that may be thorny and without a promise of fruit
Gently persevere in your effort and be resolute but kind
And never ever under estimate the power of your mind

Throw your stone skywards to pierce the shroud of darkness
Where ignorance and bigotry dwell in its primordial vastness
Throw your stone to pierce the dark shroud of the night
Use your mind and not your might to spread the power of light

Mirror Images—Life and Death

Love and death both come uninvited
No prior notice of time or place
It just happens
Fighting the inevitable changes not

Accept it without condition
Love is unconditional
How can death be conditional
There never is a right time

Fight will only increase anguish
Smile when death knocks on your door
Just as when love knocks on your door
Destiny is never charted

With smile death is vanquished
With smile love is immortalized
How can death be victorious
When love is everlasting

Smile on for love's sake

Memories of Bygone Days

Asmini scent permeating the tropical night air
Firefly flying without an earthly care
Mother's gentle song soothing my mind
Peace of the bygone days now so difficult to find

Barking of the dog chasing a critter of the night
Quietly foraging his prey in thick grass quite out of sight
Frantic whimpering of the newborn puppies for more milk
Quieted by their mother's nudging nose soft as silk

A streaking star blazing a trail of light
Surrendering its light to the dark of the night
Crickets singing a cacophony of tunes
Relating their nightly stories of many past moons

Emerging morning sun bringing back renewed light
One more day of leisure spent in my mother's sight
Her gentle reminder not to waste the light
To read and learn each day to reach a newer height

Now old and gray yearning to hear her familiar voice
Life's journey has offered much except this choice
To hear her soothing voice again once more
Surely she awaits me as I walk through the eternal door

"Mind's Eye" takes us to a land where past memories live. Mine returns to our childhood home in Tanga, Tanganyika—the memory of sounds, sight and fragrance live forever.

Moti Behan—My Older Sister

On her birthday

Age is a recurring number each year
A year of wondrous, kind thoughts
A year of things done
A year of friends and friendships

Each year showered with love that is part of my life
The longer you live the greater your gift of love
Live long and healthy
May your love be eternally mine

Mother

I searched for heaven, far and wide
I walked the burning desert sands with no water by my side
In jungles of Africa I sought
I searched for heaven and I found it not

I sat in solitude, night and day
The sage beckoned me to kneel and pray
I searched for heaven and I found it not
In vain for heaven I sought

Lost, tired, and haggard, I returned to my mother's home
I searched in Mecca, Medina, Gangotri, Bethlehem, and Rome
Tears of dejection I constantly fought
I searched for heaven and I found it not

I washed my hands to eat my mother's food
Her love and understanding calmed my mood
As she walked away, my eyes followed her feet
Beneath her feet heavenly light lit

I knew thence my heaven was at my mother's feet

Battles We Fight

We fight battles that we cannot win
Only for reasons to fight
Gold, oil, land, race, color of the skin, and religion
Reasons exhausted, we find more

God made this world for men and beast
He did not create boundaries
He did not give ownership of one over other
His book does not preach death and destruction

Drones and bombs are not his weapons
He preaches caring and sharing
Not swords but plow shears
His world is of peace not war

The Eternal Language

Setting sun celebrating yet another glorious day
Crimson sky painted with a brush-stroke of a fleeting ray
Gentle breeze enhancing the lucent glow of twilight
A symphony of bird songs nesting for the night

Finch's evening song beckoning her brood to the nest
Daylong work and tired wings just about ready to rest
Raccoon now awakened from a daylong slumber
Stretching its limbs to make them limber

First-Line Index

A

Age is a recurring number each year, 87
Amaajee we have enjoyed your shade
for many years, 57
As I first stood up to walk my parents
held my hand, 78
As night creeps in, hidden fears
awaken, 49

B

Birthstones, crosses, incense, sage weed,
lavender, candles, and *diyas*, 51
Brig. Gen. Reginald Edward Harry
Dyer's Forty-Fifth Infantry
Brigade marched, 28

C

A chance to know you better now
remains in vain, 71
Countless innocent lives lost in war, 38

D

Divergent path away from home, 69
Driving life's journey, 80

E

Each day spent in toil, 82
Each day spent toiling to dig the well
deeper, 60
Each step unfolding its own story, 56

Each turn I took, 13
Eyes searching the horizon, 31

F

Fragrant gentle breeze of fresh
blossoms, 54
The fruit tree stood its ground against
raging winds and rain, 58

G

Guru, how can I repay you for this
knowledge? 19

H

Have you felt blood boil in your veins?
83

I

I am who I am, 74
I fought the destiny that spelled your
coming, 17
If there exists a disbelief in your word,
46
If you hear a knock on your door but
find no one, 53
I have traveled far and wide stopping
from place to place, 45
In the quiet of my life I see with the
eye of my soul, 12
In your arms I touched the heavens, 73
I searched for heaven far and wide, 88

General Index

About The Author

Onaly A. Kapasi was born in Mombasa, a sleepy coastal town in Kenya. He travelled to Boston, Massachusetts form Nairobi, Kenya in 1975 for a Harvard Orthopaedic Fellowship at the Boston Children's Hospital Medical Center.

Oni, as he is fondly known, does not believe that he is a poet, but accepts that he loves writing poetry.

He is a real Boston Brahmin, living in Boston, loving and valuing Vedic principals and heritage.

He enjoys medical charity work in Boston, Africa and in India, where he cosponsors and frequently visits a free clinic in the Himalayan town of Mandi.

Poetry is his passion. These days he is more often invited to recite personal poems than give medical talks. He wishes that his readers share his joy in these poems.

Onaly A. Kapasi, MD
Arthroscopy & Sports Medicine
80 Bridge Street, on the Charles
Dedham, MA 02026
www.MassOrtho.com

Edwards Brothers Malloy
Thorofare, NJ USA
June 12, 2014